DECISIONS

DECISIONS

JACK ROEDA

BIBLE WAY
Grand Rapids, Michigan

ILLUSTRATIONS BY CHUCK SPITTERS

Library of Congress Cataloging in Publication Data

Roeda, Jack, 1945-
   Decisions.

   Bibliography: p.
   SUMMARY: Examines each of the Ten Commandments and their implications for Christian ethics and moral decision making.
   1. Commandments, Ten. 2. Christian ethics—Christian Reformed authors. [1. Ten commandments. 2. Christian life] I. Spitters, Charles. II. Title.
BV4655.R575   241.5'2   80-19628
ISBN 0-933140-14-2

First printing, 1980
Second printing, 1982

Multitudes, multitudes,
in the valley of decision!
JOEL 3:14

Contents

Contents

Preface

*This is a book on ethics. It tries to
explain what each of us ought to do in
our day-to-day living. Everything we do
has a moral or ethical side to it, just as everything has a physical, economic, or social
side. Going out on a date takes physical
energy, costs money, and requires social skills. It also
involves some moral questions. That
moral side of life is what this book discusses.
More specifically this is a book on Christian ethics. It
considers* ought *matters from the viewpoint of Christian faith
and answers moral questions in terms of Chris-
tian principles. In other words, it tries to ex-
plain what you as a Christian ought to do and why you ought to do it.
This book is part of a course by the same name,* Decisions.
*The course has two interweaving
parts: this book which teaches the basic
ethical principles and a series of case studies (most of
which were written and researched by Dan Vander Ark
of Holland, Michigan) which give you a chance
to apply those principles to real life
situations. Together they're intended to teach
you how to make right moral decisions even
in difficult and confusing circumstances.
The course, in turn, is part of a curriculum
of church education,* The Bible Way,
*published by the Education Department
of the Christian Reformed Church.
Within that curriculum* Decisions *is in-*

*tended for young adults: juniors in
high school and older.
You should find this small book
helpful by itself. It gives a good overview
of Christian morality. Following the
general order of the Ten Commandments, it
talks about some of the problems we
meet when we try to obey
those laws and illustrates what it says with interesting,
down-to-earth stories. You should
find the book both easy to read and well worth reading.
The author, Rev. Jack Roeda, is pastor of the
Calvary Christian Reformed Church in Holland,
Michigan. Following his graduation from Calvin College
and Seminary, Rev. Roeda did additional work at the Seminary,
studying under Dr. Henry Stob, to earn a masters degree in ethics.
The illustrations are by Mr. Charles Spitters. He's a
graduate of Kendall School of Design and worked for a time
as a free-lance artist out of Kalamazoo,
Michigan. Now he's art editor with
the Education Department.
This book is offered with the hope that it may help you,
the reader, see something of
how the love and law of God combine
to guide us in making moral decisions and how
such decisions should help us glorify
God in all our living.
Harvey A. Smit, Director of Education*

The Rusty Robot

CHAPTER 1

Somewhere in a forgotten corner of Africa a missionary was hard at work trying to convert the chief of a fierce tribe. The chief was very old, and the missionary leaned heavily on the "don'ts" of the Bible. After listening patiently, the chief at last said: "I do not understand. You tell me I must not take my neighbor's wife?" The missionary nodded his head in agreement. "Nor may I take his ivory or his oxen?" "Exactly!" "And I must not dance the war dance and then ambush him?" "Absolutely not!" "But I am *unable* to do any of these things," said the chief sadly. "I am too old. To be old and to be Christian— they must be the same thing."

(Joy Davidman,
*Smoke on the Mountain**)

Unfortunately many people would agree with the African chief. To them Christianity is a rigid system of dos and don'ts that takes the fun out of living. To them saints are people who live behind pinched, tight-lipped faces. To them the Christian life is nothing but rules, rules, rules.

But like the African chief, these people are mistaken. Obeying rules, following a moral code, is not the same as obeying Christ. Even if our conduct is perfect by human standards, we may be strangers to Christ. We may be obeying rules simply because our parents make us or our community expects it—because of the pressure people put on us. And when the pressure is off, the behavior usually changes.

Not long after Sally's wedding people began missing her in church. As a child and a teenager she had attended the small, conservative church with her family. It soon became apparent, however, that Sally and her husband were going hard after all the world had to offer, and God and the church had no part in their new life-style. The minister called on them several times. Once when Sally was home alone he told her that what puzzled him was how easily she was dismissing all that she had been taught as a child. "You dismiss it," he said, "as if it were nothing more than excess baggage. Good riddance! Did it never

*From *Smoke on the Mountain*, by Joy Davidman. Copyright © 1953, 1954, by Joy Davidman. Used by permission of the Westminster Press.

mean anything more to you? Anything at all?"

Sally's case isn't unusual. Before her marriage she obeyed rules, rules, rules—followed a moral code—but she did it for the wrong reasons. Pleasing parents, friends, and neighbors is important, but such behavior isn't Christian unless we feel personally responsible to God. That kind of personal relationship is the beginning of spiritual maturity.

And it's in the context of that personal relationship that God gives us his laws—laws for our own good. It's a mistake to suppose that God gave his laws so we might win his love by obeying them. Equally mistaken is the idea that he gave his laws to keep us from enjoying life. We can be sure that God is delighted to see his children happy. After all, he made this world in such a way that the very necessities of life—eating, drinking, sleeping, reproducing—are positively delightful. No, God's purpose in giving us the law is for our good.

Suppose you are a scientist and you have just constructed a marvelously complex robot. It can talk, see, even think; it is as nearly human as a machine can be. Along with many other instructions, you tell the robot not to get wet. Having made the robot, you know that water will destroy it.

One day, as the robot is taking a stroll, it sees some boys and girls playing and swimming on the beach. It watches. The children sound as if they are having great fun. Of course the robot remembers your instructions not to get wet. But the longer it watches, the more enjoyable the water looks. The robot wonders how something that appears so pleasant can hurt, and it starts to think that you are just a killjoy. Once that thought has crossed its computer, the robot moves toward the playing children who are calling it to join them. The robot dives into the water.

It has a good time. But an hour later it begins to notice that its joints are creaking, that moving is getting more difficult, and that its thinking is less than clear.

The beautiful robot is becoming rusty; it has water in its computers.

Like the scientist's instructions to the robot, God's laws are meant to show us how best to live. Their purpose is to protect us from doing and suffering evil and, more positively, to give us guidance in loving our neighbor. All God's commandments are summed up in this one rule: love. Love God above all and your neighbor as yourself (Matt. 22:37-39). This command is the heart of our moral life with God; obedience to it requires *doing*, not just feeling. If we love God and our neighbor, we will "act justly and . . . love mercy" (Mic. 6:8, NIV).

How do we act justly? We recognize that our neighbors have rights, that they are to be treated with respect. In other words, we cannot use our neighbors as means to our own personal ends.

Ken is an extremely bright student. To all other students he is the epitome of a bookworm. Ken has no close friends. Bert, on the other hand, has loads of friends, is a first-rate athlete, but has trouble with his grades. In fact, he is in danger of being taken off the basketball team. Bert's friends suggest that they call Ken, "befriend" him, and have him help Bert in his studies. Bert takes the advice.

Jim hears that Nancy is "pretty wild" on dates. He has seen her around school on several occasions and was not impressed one way or another. But he calls her for a date anyway.

How do we love mercy or kindness? We recognize that every person—whether friend or enemy, relative or stranger—is worthy of our sympathetic consideration. Sometimes that consideration is hard to remember and even harder to show. It might help if we consider every moral situation as if it involved someone dear to us. For example:

It is your sister who wants to buy the car with the faulty transmission. Should you, the seller, tell?

It is your younger brother who gets caught with the marijuana. Should you, the judge, give a jail sentence?

Our Lord does not tell us to condone evil, but he does demand that we treat everyone—including wrongdoers—with sympathetic consideration.

In New York a man is accused of killing three young women. Every day a police car takes him from the prison to the courthouse. Outside the courthouse a large crowd gathers. When the police appear with the prisoner, the crowd begins to shout and curse. One man shouts above the rest: "Give me ten minutes alone with that animal." Everyone screams approval.

Everyone but God. His command to those who would follow him remains firm: act justly and love mercy. To guide us in these fundamental tasks, God gives us guidelines. He demands that we do not dishonor our parents, that we be faithful to our marriage partner, that we do not kill anyone, that we do not lie to anyone or about anyone, and that we do not steal or look at what belongs to others with jealous eyes.

These "do nots" represent the bare minimum requirements of love. Christians, especially in the Reformed tradition, have understood that these negative commands are to be "positivised" and deepened as Jesus does in his Sermon on the Mount. To love our neighbor, therefore, not only means that we are forbidden to kill him but, as the Heidelberg Catechism says:

God tells us
  to love our neighbor as ourselves,
  to be patient, peace-loving, gentle,
    merciful, and friendly to him,
  to protect him from harm as much as we can,
  and to do good even to our enemies.

(Answer 107)

In the Valley of Decision

CHAPTER 2

It is war. Poland, Holland, Belgium, and France have surrendered to the Nazi war machine. England is the next target. With terrible fury the Nazi air force sends its bombers to blast England into submission. London is in flaming shambles. But England will not surrender.

On the fourteenth of November, German high command orders an attack on the beautiful city of Coventry, population nearly a quarter of a million. Through the darkness they come. The droning of engines shatters the stillness, air raid sirens scream out their warning—too late. The bombs explode, leaving a deathly quiet over the city. Seventy thousand homes are leveled to the ground. Thousands of men, women, and children who did not make it to the air raid shelter lay dead. The beautiful ancient churches of Coventry are smashed and scarred. England weeps.

Prime Minister Churchill comes to inspect the damages. With a stern face, cigar clenched between

Q. WHAT DO WE DO THAT IS GOOD?

A. Only that which
arises out of true faith,
conforms to God's law,
and is done for his glory;
and not that which is based
on what we think is right
or on established human tradition.

Heidelberg Catechism Q & A 91

his teeth, he walks among the ruins. He listens as the people of Coventry describe the horror of the night. He asks questions. But he tells no one his secret. He tells no one that he knew the bombing raid was coming—that he could have evacuated the city's doomed population in time.

Why would Churchill, the leader of his nation, allow his people to die when an early warning might have saved them? Because of Project Ultra—one of the most important and closely guarded secrets of World War II. Somehow Allied leaders had gotten ahold of a German code machine and had learned to decipher any message sent by the German military command. The code was extremely difficult, but they had finally cracked it. From this code Churchill received the fateful message: Coventry will be bombed.

And because of this code, because of Project Ultra, the Prime Minister faced a stark dilemma: what should he do with the information? He could order the city to be evacuated immediately, have the Royal Air Force jam the navigational aids the Germans used, and take other counter measures. But doing any of these things would tell the Germans that the Allies had advance knowledge of the attack. As a precaution they would very likely change their code system and gone would be the one great advantage the Allies had over Germany. Again and again this access to German military orders had proved to be the only thing between the Allies and defeat. Project Ultra saved the Allied forces from total destruction before Dunkirk and it gave the Royal Air Force time to get their planes off the ground before a German bombing raid. To give away the secret of Project Ultra by evacuating Coventry might mean losing the war.

Churchill agonized over the decision. In the end he decided to do nothing except to secretly put the fire fighters, police, and ambulance drivers on the alert. Human beings who could have been saved died in that raid. But it was Churchill's carefully considered opinion that to save them would endanger countless lives later and might lead to final defeat for the Allies.

Our moral decisions are rarely, if ever, so painfully difficult as this one. We usually know what we *ought* to do and what God's will requires. But there are times when, like Churchill, we too need to consider the alternatives and weigh the consequences of our decisions.

Why is moral decision making sometimes so difficult? For several reasons, one of which is ignorance. We often must act without fully knowing or understanding all possible consequences. Churchill, for example, could only *assume* that the whole war effort would be threatened if Project Ultra were found out. In the same way, when Henry Ford decided to produce his Model T, he could not look into the future and see what effect his car would have on air pollution, Middle East politics, family life, and backseat necking. Today we must make decisions about nuclear energy, disarmament, biological engineering, and countless other problems which are so complicated that it's difficult for us to get the facts straight. We have to *try*, but ignorance clouds our ability to see clearly and make clear-cut decisions.

Another barrier we face in decision making is human limitation. We must choose between competing obligations.

Ⅱt is the evening before final exams. Sue is studying when the phone rings. It's Rachel and she's terribly depressed. She says she's thinking of quitting school, leaving home . . . and maybe worse. She begins to cry and asks Sue if she can come over and talk. Sue looks at her chemistry books; there's a lot she still has to cover.
Then she hears Rachel's plea: "Will you come, Sue?"
"I'll be there in half an hour."

Like Sue, we are finite, limited. We cannot be in two places at once: we must weigh competing obligations. Like Churchill, we are ignorant of some of the consequences of our actions. Both of these problems complicate decision making. But the basic, underlying reason for our difficulty is *sin*. Sin constantly muddies the waters and introduces us to bewildering situations. Sin is responsible for a world in which police carry guns and Christians pay taxes which build atomic weapons. Sin complicates our decision making. In a faraway land government officials confiscate part of the food given to relieve the hungry and sell it on the black market. What is our responsibility? At home, the man you marry becomes vicious and cruel to you and the children. What do you do?

Some people have come up with easy answers to questions like these. They recognize that in our broken world we are asked to do things—to lie, kill, disobey authority—which we would never have to consider doing in a perfect world. But they have no problems with such behavior as long as it's "done in love." For them the Ten Commandments are merely helpful guidelines.

What about disobeying part of God's law? No problem, followers of this new morality claim. You can lie, commit adultery, steal, and even kill if you do it in love.

For obvious reasons, this approach can lead to devastating results. A recent television talk show featured an interview with several sex surrogates—women who work in a sex clinic. Their job: acting as temporary sex partners for men who are trying to overcome sexual difficulties. When asked about the morality of their work, the women answered that they were helping these men. It was the loving thing to do. "And each man [and woman] does what is right [and loving] in his [or her] own heart."

Such love is not the answer to our moral dilemmas. Instead of recognizing God as a just God, it makes him seem like a pushover who will tolerate anything. He will not. The laws he gave us form boundaries in which he expects and requires us to live. True, sometimes in emergency situations when we face genuinely conflicting duties, it may be necessary to step across the boundary of one of God's laws in order to be obedient to another. For instance, you tell a lie to hide the Jew from the Nazi soldier. But under normal circumstances, disobedience to God's law is inexcusable.

The trouble today is that we stroll outside the area set by God's laws with altogether too much ease. We lie about our age to get into the amusement park at half price. We disobey our parents because they are old-fashioned. We cheat on our income tax because "the government owes us." We live unchaste lives because it feels good.

Our first unmistakable duty is to obey the laws of God. In the book *Lest Innocent Blood Be Shed* we read the story of the French pastor, André Trocmé. Wanted by the Gestapo police for his work among the Jewish refugees, he was caught, quite by accident, in a railroad station.

Sitting in the barred vehicle, he mustered his thoughts. His identity card gave his name as Béguet, and they would ask him if this was indeed true. Then he would have to lie in order to hide his identity. But he was not able to lie; lying, especially to save his own skin, was "sliding toward those compromises that God had not called upon me to make," he wrote in his autobiographical notes on the incident.

He decided that when the German police questioned him, he would say, "I am not Monsieur Béguet, I am pastor André Trocmé." Having made this decision, he became calm; his conscience was quiet.

We are God's people. He sets the boundaries of our lives and burdens us with the welfare of our neighbor. In this fallen world love must seek what is the most good we can do—and the least evil.

BEFORE THE NAME
GOES ON

CHAPTER 3

"You shall not take the name of the Lord your God in vain; for the Lord will not hold him guiltless who takes his name in vain."

The Third Commandment

Two tourists, an American and a Canadian, were traveling across England by train. After studying her fellow passengers, the American nudged the Canadian and whispered: "Do you see the man sitting five seats ahead of us? I think he's the Archbishop of Canterbury. I recognize him from pictures in the paper and on television." "I don't think so," the Canadian replied, carefully studying the passenger in question. "In fact, I'm sure you're mistaken."

An argument followed, both tourists insisting they were right. Finally the Canadian challenged: "Look, if you're so sure, why don't you talk to him?" "I will," the American replied stonily.

As the Canadian watched, her friend eased her way up the aisle to the man she had identified as leader of the Church of England. "Excuse me, sir," she said respectfully, "but my friend and I were wondering whether you are the Archbishop of Canterbury. I say you are."

The passenger, resenting the intrusion, glared up at the tourist. Swearing loudly and angrily he told her to mind her own blankety-blank business. Surprised by the outburst, the American quickly returned to her seat.

"Well, *is* he the Archbishop of Canterbury?" the Canadian asked. "I don't know," answered the puzzled American. "He wouldn't say."

Would an archbishop swear to disguise his identity? Probably not. At least one would hope not. While disguise may be a way of life for film stars and spies, the church has no need for subterfuge. If God had called us to be plain-clothes persons, undercover agents, we would blend with the rest of the world—lying, swearing, injuring, and dishonoring as they do. But he didn't. He called us to be clothed with "compassion, kindness, humility, gentleness and patience" (Col. 3:12, NIV). He called us to live lives that will honor and praise his name.

Unfortunately we do not always succeed. We pray, as Jesus taught us, that God's name be hallowed; but often we're responsible for dragging it through the dirt. We want to show the world how excellent our God is, but sometimes we give them the opposite impression. Old Testament Israel made that mistake too. They disgraced God's name among the nations by living sinfully (Ezek. 36:16-35). Their conduct caused people to lose respect for God just as you would lose respect for a school that consistently graduated illiterates. Saying "hallowed be thy name" is not enough; our lives speak louder than our words.

George had a weakness. Everyone knew. He liked his alcohol too much. Every so often he could be seen staggering along the town's main street. Both the minister and the elders had talked to George about his problem, and he admitted that it was wrong. He even promised to stop. However, usually after a couple of weeks the whole town would be buzzing again about how George had put it away the night before.

It couldn't go on. At the next elders' meeting several spoke on the matter. "It's disgraceful," one elder said. "His behavior is scandalous," said another. "For the purity of the church and the honor of God's name we must do some-thing," concluded the pastor. That very night they decided to begin disciplinary action—a procedure that would end either in George's repentance or his excommunication from the church.

Unholy and inconsistent Christian living is a discredit to God. Yet it is not just the Georges in the church who ruin God's reputation. At least George was always ashamed and troubled by what he did—he knew he was a sinner. Countless others—the nominal Christians—do not. They use the name "Christian" but are as worldly, as self-seeking, and as guilty of petty dishonesty as any unbeliever. They call themselves "Christian" but live for that fancy car or speak about people of other races with contempt. Their ungodly living convinces unbelievers that religion is useless—and embarrasses God. At times God must feel the way parents feel when Junior acts like a spoiled brat in a crowded restaurant.

Using the name Christian carries responsibilities. Some years ago a commercial used as its slogan: "Before the name goes on, the quality goes in." That's a good slogan for the church. Just as the name of the company is damaged if the quality of its products is poor, so the name of God is damaged if the quality of his products—Christians—is poor. "Before the name goes on, the quality must go in." And if we have no intention of living Christlike lives, then we ought not to call ourselves by Christ's name.

What kind of living hallows God's name? Living that reflects an overriding desire to be a credit to God. Of course, at times there will be inconsistencies—we will fall short; but we have to keep striving to honor God. Because he is pure, loving, faithful, and just, he expects us to reflect those qualities. That means turning away from foul conversation, loving people who hurt us or hate us, being dependable and true to our word, hating injustice—all of these actions honor God.

It made the headlines in the local paper. The Allen Company was giving $250,000 to the local Christian college. It was a much needed boost in the college's expansion program. Several years before the same company had given a brand-new airplane to the mission station in Zaire. On the day the gift of $250,000 became public, the paper's editorial praised the company for its community spirit. The pastor visited the Allens personally to show his approval of their generosity.

But Jill Anderson, who works on the assembly line at Allen's, had a different perspective. After she read the news, she grumbled: "I just wish they would pay their employees more than minimum wage requires."

If we are going to be successful in honoring God, we must be holy in *all* that we do (I Pet. 1:15). Gifts to a Christian college and an African mission field are fine gestures, but they are not enough. Our Christianity must be more than skin-deep or it is not real. In every part of our lives we must obey God's command: "Be holy because I am holy."

That's a difficult thought for some of us. Holiness has received a lot of bad press and, as a result, being holy has little appeal. We've all heard misguided descriptions of the holy life: holiness is a long list of dos and don'ts; holiness is going to Bible study class on Wednesday evening and asking everyone on Sunday why they weren't there; holiness is a life without laughter; holiness means attending all the prayer meetings and spiritual growth seminars within a one hundred mile radius. That's what the world thinks. To them holy people are pinch-faced, self-righteous, and spiritually conceited.

But they're wrong. Holy lives are lives set apart for God, lives dedicated to God, distinguished by their moral beauty. Do you remember Copernicus, the sixteenth century astronomer? He taught that the universe was not geocentric, but heliocentric. It is the sun, he said, and not our earth that stands at the center around which everything else revolves. His theory, which astounded the world, is called the Copernican revolution. In a sense, holiness is another "Copernican revolution"—a revolution that takes place not in our physical world but in our spiritual and moral world. God is the center around which the self, the home, and the nation revolve. Self-centered living is out.

Mother Teresa, a Catholic nun who worked for years among the poorest of the poor in the slums of Calcutta, won the 1979 Nobel Peace Prize. The widespread attention, television coverage, and fame which she received as a prize winner, however, did not change Mother Teresa's attitude. In a television interview she confessed: "I am only a little pencil in the hand of God."

That is holiness—a life wholly at God's disposal. But it's not easy to live that kind of life. Unlike Mother Teresa most of us have a lot of trouble detaching ourselves from the world and its things. It's no secret that the passion for owning things is one of the driving forces behind our feverish world. Like the fool in Jesus' parable, people spend their whole lives filling up their barns.

Louie is a senior at Riggsfield High. Every day, both before and after school, you can find him "cruising" around school in his sports car. Sometimes he picks up some other students and they slowly wind their way through town looking tough.

To Louie the car is everything. He worked and saved all through his first three years of high school to buy it. Now he spends all of his spare time waxing, polishing, and adorning it with new gadgets. Louie has his identity wrapped up in the car. He is possessed by his possession.

Being possessed by possessions, lenient about immorality, tolerant of injustice—all of these keep us from living holy lives that honor God. It's difficult to put all of our possessions—our whole life—at God's disposal. But we must keep trying.

In New Eyes for Invisibles Rufus Jones retells an old legend about a company of horse riders who traveled through a mysterious land in the dark of night. As they crossed a dry river bed, they heard a voice: "Take a handful of the pebbles from the river bed and you will be both glad and sad." Each rider did as the voice commanded; then they continued their journey in the dark. When the morning finally came and they were bathed in the light of the sun, one of the travelers remembered the strange command. The riders reached into their pockets and pulled out the pebbles. To their amazement they saw that the stones were in fact diamonds and rubies and sapphires. Then they were both glad and sad—glad that they had taken some pebbles and sad that they had not taken more.

On the day of judgment we shall be glad we brought honor to God and sad that we did not bring more. "Our Father in heaven, hallowed be thy name" through us.

Together

CHAPTER 4

On Sunday morning Mr. and Mrs. Invisible Religion sit down to watch "church." They are impressed by the highly professional preacher with the fetching smile. They are thrilled by the celebrities talking about themselves under the guise of born-again autobiographies. They are entertained by the pink-tuxedoed men and the low-necklined women caressing microphones among spurting fountains. And they are certain their "electronic church" is far preferable to services in that ancient building down the street.

And why not? Why should they give up their smooth Hollywood service for a seat in a crowded pew with a congregation of real believers, sinners, off-key choirs, sweaty and homely people who need them, people they do not like but are supposed to love? Why should they give up professional, polished sermons (which they can switch off at will) to listen to ordinary pastors who preach grace along with calls to discipleship, who make awkward,

Q. What is God's will for us in the fourth commandment?

A. . . . That, especially on the festive day of rest, I regularly attend the assembly of God's people. . . .

Heidelberg Catechism, Q & A 103

sometimes offensive, pleas for stewardship?

(Adapted from Martin Marty, "The Electronic Church")

Why indeed? The majority in our society would agree that Mr. and Mrs. Invisible Religion have no need of the traditional church. Church, to these people, is a bore and a nuisance. If they have to attend a service at all, they prefer to do it in the privacy of their own living rooms over bowls of breakfast cereal. But church—that building full of straight-laced, somber-faced people—is definitely out.

If you would give these people a multiple choice quiz on religion, many of them would answer as follows:

1. There is a God. . . . .(Yes) No
2. God is concerned
   about people. . . . .(Yes) No
3. God is creator, judge,
   redeemer . . . .(Yes) No
4. God is revealed in
   Jesus Christ. . . . .(Yes) No

5. God demands obedience . . . (Yes) No
6. One who believes these things
   must be active in the church . . Yes (No)

(R. Brown, *The Bible Speaks to You*)

God—yes. Church—no. And we have all heard their arguments:

"Where does it say in the Bible that you have to go to church?"

"Do you mean to tell me that if I don't go to church, I won't go to heaven?"

"I think religion is a personal matter between God and me."

"I get a lot more out of a quiet walk in the woods than sitting in a stuffy building."

"The minister is boring."

"I don't believe God keeps office hours."

"The church is full of hypocrites."

It is true, of course, that the Sunday worship service can be disappointing, hardly a time of renewal. The service is sometimes dull. The music isn't our kind of music. The preacher talks and sometimes shouts over our heads. And when these things happen we become impatient. We know we aren't in church to learn the virtue of patience, to practice long-suffering, or to master the art of sitting still. But why *are* we there? Could Mr. and Mrs. Invisible Religion be right? Is it possible (and maybe preferable) to remain a Christian without attending church?

Our answer to that question really depends on what we think it means to be a Christian. If we think that Christianity is a private matter between God and the soul, then we might very well replace the local church with a good book, an inspiring record, or even a TV worship service. But such an approach quickly runs into problems. The Bible describes Christians as parts of a body, none of which can function without the other:

The eye cannot say to the hand, "I don't need you!" And the head cannot say to the feet, "I don't need you." On the contrary, those parts of the body that seem to be weaker are indispensable, and the parts that we think are less honorable we treat with special honor.

Now you are the body of Christ, and each of you is a part of it.

(I Cor. 12:21-23, 27 NIV)

It's just not possible to be a Christian all alone. " . . . Being a Christian by yourself (without the church) is like trying to play tennis by yourself. It's like trying to be a glowing coal separated from the rest of the embers. Your little light will go out (C. Plantinga Jr., *A Place to Stand*). To keep our light from dying, we must gather together, as a body or a community. From Monday through Saturday members of that community are scattered throughout society—studying geometry, managing stores, keeping house. But on Sunday the community reassembles—Christians gather for worship.

And it's very important that we attend these gatherings. During the week it's easy to lose sight of who we are.

A group of American explorers traveled to Africa, hoping to see as much of that continent as possible. They hired native guides and enthusiastically began hiking into that wild and unknown land. The first day they rushed, and they rushed again on the second day, the third day, and every day. But on the seventh day they ran into problems. They were packed and ready to rush some more when they noticed their guides were not cooperating; they were sitting under a tree. "Come on," the explorers shouted. But the guides shook their heads. "We no go today," they said. "We rest today to let our souls catch up with our bodies."

(Adapted from Charles Allen, *God's Psychiatry*)

It may sound ridiculous to our scientific twentieth century minds, but what the guides said reflects a lot of wisdom. Like them, we must take one day in seven to "let our souls catch up with our bodies." A week in the factory may leave us feeling tired and empty. A week of tests, quizzes, and homework may make us ask what direction we are taking. A week of television, government scandal, and rising inflation may make us feel skeptical and hopeless. But on Sunday we are reminded that we are not alone: we hear God calling, reminding us that we are his redeemed people and that we belong together.

Knowing this—knowing that we *need* the Sunday worship service to get ourselves and our relationship to God and community in proper perspective—we may overlook some of the deficiencies of the Sunday gathering and look to all that it does for us. Every member of the community comes to church with individual needs. They come together to celebrate their redemption, to have communion with each other, and to listen to God speak.

Some of them are hoping for a service which will make them "feel good all over." Others look for a service which will "pep them up, interest them." Still others like the service best when there is a good deal of shouting about "fire and brimstone," when the preacher pounds the pulpit denouncing the sins in Ottawa and Washington D.C. In *Travels with Charley,* the well-known American author, John Steinbeck, tells of his experience at a fire-and-brimstone church.

Sunday morning, in a Vermont town . . . I shaved, dressed in a suit, polished my shoes, whited my sepulcher, and looked for a church to attend. Several I eliminated for reasons I do not now remember, but on seeing a John Knox church, I drove into a side street and parked. . . . I took my seat in the rear of the spotless polished place of worship. The prayers were to the point, directing the attention of the Almighty to certain weaknesses and undivine tendencies I know to be mine and could only suppose were shared by others gathered there.

The service did my heart and I hope my soul some good. It had been long since I had heard such an approach. It is our practice now, at least in the large cities, to find from our psychiatric priesthood that our sins aren't really sins at all but accidents that are set in motion by forces beyond our control. There was no such nonsense in this church. The minister, a man of iron with tool-steel eyes and a delivery like a pneumatic drill, opened up with prayer and reassured us that we were a pretty sorry lot. And he was right. We didn't amount to much to start with, and due to our own tawdry efforts we have been slipping ever since. Then, having softened us up, he went into a glorious sermon, a fire-and-brimstone sermon. Having proved that we, or perhaps only I, were no damn good, he painted with cool certainty what was likely to happen to us if we didn't make some basic reorganizations for which he didn't hold out much hope. He spoke of hell as an expert, not the mush-mush hell of these soft days, but a well-stoked, white-hot hell served by technicians of the first order. This reverend brought it to a point where we could understand it, a good hard coal fire, plenty of draft, and a squad of open-hearth devils who put their hearts into their work, and their work was me. I began to feel good all over. For some years now God has been a pal to us, practicing togetherness, and that causes . . . emptiness. But this Vermont God cared . . . about me. He put my sin in a new perspective.

(John Steinbeck,
*Travels with Charley**)

Whatever our needs, the Sunday service *does* give us that new perspective. There's something more to a service than "enjoying" it and being made "to feel good all over." During that worship hour God touches our souls: the divine reality becomes real for us. And the result may be, should be, very practical.

Whatever we're looking for, the Sunday service gives us a new look. Not perhaps that we look different to others, but they look different to us. We see them in a new way. God doesn't look like that kind old man "up there," but like the holy, mighty, gracious Creator and Sustainer of all life. Jesus doesn't look like a remarkably humble and good teacher, but like the Savior and Lord of all people. Neighbors don't look like statistics or high-bred animals with clever brains, but like God's image-bearers.

Faith is like glasses. Perched on our noses, often awkward and insecure, they still help us see things we couldn't before. They give us a new look at life.

But glasses get dirty, soiled, and greasy. Soon we're not seeing clearly again. Things get blurred and murky. They need, obviously, regular cleaning and polishing. They need normal maintenance.

Sunday worship is a sort of faith maintenance. Faith's vision gets blurred by our selfishness, smudged by our petty sins, soiled by our contact with evil. The Sunday worship resharpens our vision, redirects our attention, realigns our perspectives, and reinforces our proper attitudes. It corrects our nearsighted fascination with our own feelings or our farsighted utopian gaze at some great ideal. It makes us see clearly our neighbor in need, opportunities for service, and our oneness with fellow believers. So on Sunday morning, our vision is cleared through

learning what God's Word teaches,
participating in the sacraments,
praying to God publicly,
and bringing Christian offerings for the
poor.

(Heidelberg Catechism, Answer 103)

An old miner once explained to a visitor, "I let my mules spend one day a week outside the mines to keep them from going blind" (Charles Allen, *God's Psychiatry*). We have the same need as those mules. Unless we spend time away from the daily grind of life, in communion with the family of God, we will go blind in our souls.

Frogs, Chickens,
and Children

CHAPTER 5

Frogs, chickens, and children—what do they have in common? Well, for one thing, they all have parents.

Of course, frogs and chickens don't pay much attention to their parents—they don't have to. Frogs never even meet their mothers and fathers, and little chicks are able to live on their own from day one. Parents, obviously, don't play a very big role in frog and chicken circles.

But you and I—for the first few months of our lives—can't even roll over. It takes us nearly a year to learn to walk. And society continues to classify us as "children" until we're eighteen.

Why do we stay "in the nest" so long? The reason isn't hard to find. It's because we have so much to learn. Growing up isn't just getting bigger and older. Our minds, our consciences, our very souls have to develop. We have to learn far more than the art of survival. We have to learn what we will be for the rest of our lives.

And pity our poor parents: thousands of diapers, temper tantrums, tens of thousands of dollars, and years of love and concern go into each child. What a job! Do you remember the tasks of Hercules, the Greek Samson? His twelve impossible feats—including cleaning a mammoth stable in one day, killing a serpent with nine heads, and capturing the monster who guarded the gates to the "lower world"—might give you some idea what people mean when

Q. What is God's will for us in the fifth commandment?

A. That I honor, love, and be loyal to my father and mother . . .
and also that I be patient with their failings. . . .

Heidelberg Catechism, Q & A 104

they say being a parent is a "herculean" job.

Of course, each parent looks at that job differently. And each child has his or her own idea of what *parent* means. For some people *parent* means dictator. Such mothers and fathers treat their children like kings and queens treat their subjects. With commanding voice and heavy hand they lay down the law and their children obey.

"Do that because I say so!"

"As long as you're in my house and eating food off my table, you'll do what I say!"

That relationship soon wears thin. The harsh shout and heavy hand may force children to walk the line, but it usually brings open hostility by young adulthood.

For other people *parent* means "buddy." Let's be friends. Such mothers and fathers feel guilty if they're not playing with their children. They don't want to force them to do anything. In religion that becomes: "We're going to let our children decide for themselves. We're not going to force our religion down their throats."

The problem with this "we're equal, we're pals" approach is that it's just not true. In experience, in knowledge, in God-given status, parents are far superior to their children, at least in early years. Intentionally or not, children take their cue about right and wrong, God and religion, from their parents.

The most helpful idea of the parent-child relationship is probably that of craftsman and apprentice. The dictionary defines an apprentice as someone "...put under the care of an employer (craftsman) for instruction in a trade." Similarly, God places us under the care of fathers and mothers for instruction in the art of living. Their job is to train us, for God. Our job is to honor them—and to allow ourselves to be taught and guided by them into the Christian life.

In this apprenticeship relation, parents are not commissioned to shape us into replicas of themselves; rather, they are to train us to become imitators of God, each according to his or her own unique gifts.

The Roeda family of eight left the Netherlands for California in the 1950s. Mr. Roeda had a dream—to have his own farm. Since he was thirteen years old, he had worked for other farmers. But in America, he heard, there were still opportunities to have your own place, work your own land. So he took his wife, his two sons, and his four daughters to a land where he planned to turn his dream into a reality.

Things didn't go quite as well as he had hoped. He worked hard, but the dairy business was expensive and difficult to get into. In fact, he had all but given up on his dream when something wonderful happened: his oldest son, Jack, graduated from high school and began milking cows full time.

When Jack started coming home with sizable paychecks, Mr. Roeda was sure the dream was in reach. One night he talked with his son about moving to the state of Washington. The land there, he pointed out, was still relatively inexpensive. Several of their acquaintances had moved there recently and were doing well. "You know, Jack," his father added, "I think the two of us could make a go of it in Washington. I know you've been wanting to go to college, but wouldn't it be great to have our own dairy farm? Together I'm sure we could manage it."

Jack looked surprised. "I'm sure we could, Dad," he said honestly, "but I'm no farmer. Nothing against cows, but I really hate milking them."

There was a brief pause. Then: "Well, give it some more thought. I just want you to be very sure," was all Mr. Roeda said.

The question never came up again; autumn came and Jack went to college. He didn't realize it at the time, but in that brief conversation his father had sacrificed a lifelong dream to allow Jack to develop his own gifts.

Not all parents succeed in being as self-sacrificing as my father. Like their children, parents are not perfect. They are themselves still beginners in the art of Christian living. They get angry over the wrong things. They forget their task as Christian mothers and fathers, lose sight of God, and get all caught up in little pointless matters.

Yet it is crucial that parents try to live the kind of lives they want their children to live. There is real trouble when parents' lives contradict what they teach. If a mother warns, "Don't lie," but thinks nothing of canceling an unwanted appointment with a false, "Sorry, I'm sick," her children will learn that lying is all right when convenient. That means parents must remember that almost everything they say and do influences their children.

And children must remember that their parents love them. When neighbors call us hopeless, our parents see a future full of possibilities. When everyone else thinks we're homely, mother sees a handsome or beautiful face. Nearly all parents think the world of their children. And it's because of that love that parents discipline us. The very things we complain about most—"they're always picking on me" or "they're always asking where I'm going and who my friends are"—are in fact expressions of our parents' love.

That loving discipline can be especially difficult for teenagers to understand. As we battle for independence, our parents seem to get in the way. Their questions and concern sound like nagging and interference. In reaction, we sometimes temporarily abandon some of the values they have taught us. We want to test and examine those values before we accept them as our own.

Karl was a teenager in Germany during the time Hitler's party took over the government. Like most of his class, he joined the Hitler Youth. His family disapproved, but he joined anyway. He knew his mother and father were upset because the group was teaching him to despise Jews. But he pointed out that Hitler Youth also made him proud to be a German. And he insisted there was no clash between being a Hitler Youth and a Christian.

One afternoon he'd been out with other Hitler Youth harassing Jews. He and his friends had upset some peddlar's carts, broken windows, and dumped merchandise in stores. When Karl came home, he was still exhilarated from the afternoon's activities. Excitedly he told his mother what they'd been doing. He told her how scared the stupid Jews had been, how funny they looked when the boys upset their carts, how some howled and others cried. He was laughing about it—proud of what they'd done.

Karl's mother looked at him strangely. Quietly she said, "Jesus was a Jew."

Just that. But suddenly Jews weren't funny anymore and Karl wasn't one bit proud of what they'd done. He quit the Hitler Youth that week.

Like Karl's mother, many parents must stand by and watch as their adolescents experiment with the world and its philosophies. Sometimes, like Karl, they can be drawn back with a word. But many times the period of testing is longer and more painful. As a result these are trying years for parents. Mothers and fathers hope and pray that ". . . the end of all your wandering is to come back where you started and know it for the first time" (T. S. Eliot). But they read in newspapers about the high percentage of young people into drugs, free sex, and Eastern religions. And noticing other children growing up and leaving the church, parents are afraid.

Of course, these years are trying for the teenager too. No longer children, not yet adults, they search for an identity with which they can live the rest of their lives. They experiment. Why do Mom and Dad hold on so tight? Don't they realize I'm not a little kid anymore? Don't they trust me?

Regardless of such tensions, however, God still wants us to honor our parents. In fact, honoring our parents never becomes optional.

Once upon a time there was a little old man. His eyes blinked and his hands trembled; when he ate he clattered his silverware distressingly, missed his mouth with the spoon as often as not, and dribbled a bit of his food on the tablecloth. Now he lived with his married son, having nowhere else to live, and his son's wife was a modern young woman who knew that in-laws should not be tolerated in a woman's home.

"I can't have this," she said. "It interferes with a woman's right to happiness."

So she and her husband took the little old man gently but firmly by the arm and led him to the corner of the kitchen. There they set him on a stool and gave him his food, what there was left of it, in an earthenware bowl. From then on, he always ate in the corner, blinking at the table with wistful eyes.

One day his hands trembled rather more than usual, and the earthenware bowl fell and broke.

"If you are a pig," said the daughter-in-law, "you must eat out of a trough." So they made him a little wooden trough, and he got his meals in that.

These people had a four-year-old son of whom they were very fond. One suppertime the young man noticed his boy playing with some bits of wood and asked what he was doing.

"I'm making a trough," he said, smiling for approval, "to feed you and Mamma out of when I get big."

The man and his wife looked at each other for a while and didn't say anything. Then they cried a little. Then they went back to the corner and took the little old man by the arm and led him back to the table. They sat him in a comfortable chair and gave him his food on a plate, and from then on nobody ever scolded when he clattered or spilled or broke things.

(Joy Davidman,
Smoke on the Mountain *)

A four-year-old child and a pig trough may seem exaggerated, but they teach a valuable lesson about the family. We all learn together and need to learn together, parents and children. And while we are learning, we must try to be patient and understanding.

Tensions and misunderstandings need not last forever. The more our parents recognize that we are becoming sensitive to the Word of God, the more they will trust us on our own. And when we are adults we honor our parents best when we show them that their instructions and prayers and love were not spent in vain. They were good craftsmen. They have taught us the art of Christian living, and we are grateful to them for that for the rest of our lives.

Honor your father and mother for it is through them that God seeks to rule you.

*From *Smoke on the Mountain*, by Joy Davidman. Copyright © 1953, 1954, by Joy Davidman. Used by permission of the Westminster Press.

Don't Trample the Violets

CHAPTER 6

Q. What is God's will for us in the sixth commandment?

A. I am not to belittle, insult, hate, or kill my neighbor. . . .

Heidelberg Catechism, Q & A 105

I met Violet when she was a junior in South High—and it didn't take long to see she had problems. There was certainly nothing about her appearance that would explain her sad life: she looked like an average high school student. But if you watched her nervously strut through the halls, frequently leaving disaster in her wake, you soon realized that Violet didn't fit in. Maybe it was because things were always happening to her: she fainted in P.E. class; she dropped her typewriter on the floor in typing class (probably a first in South High history); and she tripped and fell over the doormat at the main entrance to school. A living calamity—that's what Violet was. Once, while thirty grinning faces watched, nervous Violet chewed her pen so hard that ink spurted all over her face, hands, and clothes.

Few students took Violet seriously. Even in greetings she could hear the barely disguised mocking tone: "Hi, Violet" sounded more like, "Hi, fool." She told me that sometimes boys would intentionally trip her and then howl with laughter as they kicked her books out of reach.

Once, on a class outing, Violet waded into a fast-flowing stream. About halfway across, she felt the sand shifting under her feet and began screaming for help. Her classmates, assuming she was just trying to be the center of attention, began taunting her mercilessly. When she grabbed frantically at the rope they tossed her, they threw her the other end. Violet was terrified. Finally a teacher noticed the spectacle and rescued the shaking girl from the water. As the teacher scolded Violet for her foolishness, her classmates stood around shaking their heads. "Violet, Violet," they said scornfully.

I got to know Violet quite well. She would burst into our house, stay for only a few minutes, and then leave. But in those short visits, she said a great deal. She told me that no one loved her. I told her that wasn't so because *we* loved her. She wouldn't hear of it. And when I tried to tell her God loved her, she angrily shouted: "Prove it—just prove it!" I remember her standing by the stairway of our house and saying: "I'm nobody. I'm less than dirt." And she believed it.

Violet's parents tried to help. They took her to the parish priest. They took her to a psychiatrist. But no one could seem to erase that deeply ingrained conclusion: "I'm less than dirt."

One day Violet disappeared. She had been gone more than a week before police found her wandering the streets of a large city hundreds of miles from home. And she had an ugly story to tell. Frightened, nervous Violet had allowed men to use her sexually. Why? Because the sweet nothings they whispered in her ear—even though she knew they were lies—were better than the ridicule she received in school.

Violet. She was lonelier than any high school student ought to be. There was not one ounce of self-esteem in her. She even talked of suicide. So finally Violet was admitted to a psychiatric hospital.

Violets grow everywhere—even where you live. If you look awhile, you'll find them in your church and in your school. The Violets of this world are the girls who have no friends, the boys who are always left out. They don't think much of themselves because they're sure that no one else does. Violets are tiny and tender. It's extremely easy to ignore them or to trample on them. What they need is love and attention. And that's exactly what Christians should give them. While others taunt and trample the Violets, we must let them know they are wanted and not forgotten.

Why? Because every human being needs to think he or she is worthwhile. Violet does; you and I do. We need to hear appreciation in the tone of people's voices and we need to read it in their eyes. According to Henry Stob, "To exist means to stand out, and if a man exists he wants to stand out, even when he is not outstanding." Most of us dread being ridiculed more than being hated. When others snicker or sneer or simply ignore us, our shaky self-esteem trembles and may not soon recover. That's human. And every human life, even one that has neither talents nor attractiveness on its side, is worth preserving and protecting.

What's so special about being human? Some would locate the value of human life in the fact that it is so marvelously made. Human life, they say, is the great achievement of tens of thousands of years of evolution. Dr. Lewis Thomas, a physician and author, writes that he finds it puzzling that people make such a fuss over the test-tube baby in England. He writes:

> The true miracle was, as always, the union of egg and sperm and the emergence of a cell that can grow into a human brain. The mere existence of that cell should be one of the greatest astonishments of the earth. People ought to be walking around all day, all through their waking hours, calling out in wonderment, talking of nothing except that cell.

That cell *and* its Maker. The value of human life lies not in its breathtaking complexity but in its unique relation to God. We are made in God's image. We are greater than the stars not only because we know they are up there and they do not know we're down here, but because the Creator of those stars has stamped his image on us.

Violets must not be trampled on because God cares for them as if he had no one else in all the universe to care for. And if a human life matters that much to God, we certainly better respect, protect, and assist it. The scientist in the laboratory, the student in the classroom, the orderly in the psychiatric ward, the doctor on hospital rounds—all must be told to handle with care. Neither our own existence nor the existence of any other human being may be treated with contempt.

The visiting room is crowded with several dozen elderly men and women, some chatting with family members, others sitting in wheelchairs, staring blankly into space. The air is filled with a strong, unpleasant odor.

Fred sits in a chair, strapped in by a tray. A nurse enters the room, looks at Fred and asks: "Did you wet your pants, Fred?" She speaks unnecessarily loud. Everyone hears the question. Faces turn; the room becomes silent. Fred blushes, shakes his head, and mumbles an inaudible "no." Not satisfied the nurse reaches down to feel his pants for herself. She mutters something about letting her know when he has to go and leaves the room.

Fred lowers his head; he does not look up. Whatever dignity he felt was destroyed that afternoon.

Examples like this of contempt for human life

are numerous. Millions of abortions are performed each year; for reasons that would barely justify shooting a dog, people kill the unborn. But we need not go to the abortion clinic. Consider your school or your church. Are the Violets in your circle treated with any more respect than that lonely, frightened student was treated with in South High? Respect life! It belongs to God.

But respect is not enough. Human life must be protected—it must be shielded from destruction. And if the life of Violet shows anything, then clearly we can destroy one another without using knives and guns: we can "murder" a person by using words and looks to destroy his or her self-esteem. The old rhyme—sticks or stones may break my bones, but words will never hurt me—is false. Words can cut deeper than any sword and leave scars that last a lifetime. To obey the command not to kill we must put a watch over our mouths, speaking words that build up rather than destroy.

Human life demands our protection. Even if it is incurably sick, or senile, or deformed, we may not quietly dispose of it. The true strength of a society is to be measured in its care for its weaker members.

Is it then never right to kill another human being? The commandment rather plainly says, "Thou shalt not kill." However, those who know their Hebrew will tell you that the commandment is best translated, "Thou shalt not murder." It is always wrong to murder someone, but it is sometimes necessary to kill. It is necessary for the soldier in time of war, for the police in the line of duty, and for the doctor if the life of the unborn threatens the life of the mother. However, in all these cases the primary intention is still to protect the innocent and to stop the aggressor. We need continually to seek ways to protect human life from wanton destruction and to create a society where guns are less and less necessary.

Finally, because we recognize human life as a gift from God, we must assist it. The Heidelberg Catechism says that it is not enough that we do not kill our neighbor. "God tells us to love our neighbor as ourselves, . . . to protect him from harm as much as we can, and to do good even to our enemies" (Answer 107).

Our life is a journey from the womb to the throne room of God. It is an immense journey for such weak and feeble creatures as ourselves. Yet every human being travels it. The road can be difficult and treacherous. Some of the travelers are poorly equipped. They are weighed down with burdens.

Very brief is the time in which we can help them, in which their happiness or misery is decided. Be it ours to shed sunshine on their path, to lighten their sorrows by the balm of sympathy, to give the pure joy of a never-tiring affection, to strengthen failing courage, to instill faith in hours of despair.

(Bertrand Russell, "A Free Man's Worship")

And when the journey is finished may no one point to any of us and say: "I lived a miserable life because of him or her." Rather, may they say: "When I felt unwanted, he looked me up. When I thought life was not worth living, she treated me as a somebody."

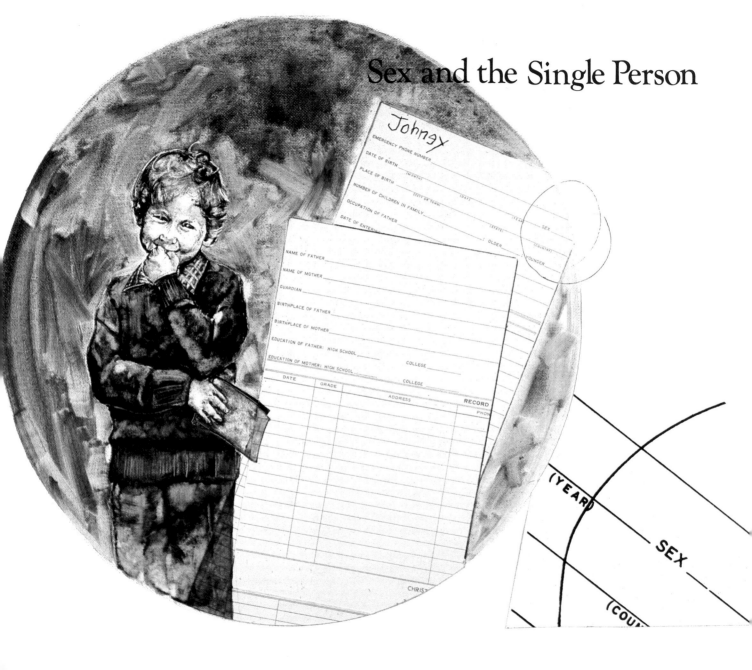

Sex and the Single Person

CHAPTER 7

*"Arise, my love, my fair one,
and come away.
. . . let me see your face,
let me hear your voice. . . ."*

Song of Solomon 2:13,14

When Johnny came home from his first day at the new school, he had a question. "Mom, what's sex?" he asked. Taken by surprise, Johnny's mother repeated the question to stall for time. She had not expected the question so soon. After all, Johnny was only in the second grade.

For a moment she hesitated, wondering what they were teaching her young son in this new school. But she was not one to shirk her duty. She sat down at the table with Johnny and began telling him about the birds and the bees, about mommies and daddies, and about all the wonderful mysteries of nature. It was a ten-minute, careful, sometimes hesitant explanation.

Johnny listened open-mouthed, obviously puzzled by his mother's words. When she had finished, he shook his head, held up his enrollment card, and asked with genuine confusion: "Boy, Mom, how do you write all that in this little square where it says SEX?"*

Most of us would have no problem filling in the SEX square on an enrollment card. We know whether we're male or female. It's the rest of it—the sexuality Johnny's mother tried to explain in second-grade language—that often leaves us confused. Few of us really know how we feel or ought to feel about our sexuality. Should we be ashamed of our fantasies and daydreams or should we exult in them? Should we condemn a television network for airing programs that promote sexual freedom, or should we congratulate them for their honesty? And how do we deal with the friend or neighbor who gambles family, career, and reputation—all for the sake of sex? Is sex as important and as powerful as it seems?

Our sexually supercharged world would answer yes. And in a way they are right: sex is powerful and it is important—but it isn't all-powerful and all-important. As Christians we have to carefully and honestly sort out our feelings about sex.

It's obvious that some attitudes toward human sexuality are wrong. The prude, for example, thinks sex is dirty, a regrettable part of our anatomy. He or she has difficulty understanding why God chose such embarrassing means to produce human beings. Fortunately, prudes are

---

*Adapted from James Dobson, *Dare to Discipline*

47

not very common today.

Opposite the prude stands the other extreme: the playboy. The playgirl and playboy view sex as an amusement ride to be enjoyed when and with whom they please. After all, they explain, sex is just a biological drive like eating and drinking. And in satisfying your thirst it doesn't really matter which glass you use.

For obvious reasons the church has more often been connected with the first attitude than with the second. According to an opinion poll, many young people are convinced that the church believes sex is a sin. But they're wrong. True, there have been some muddle-headed Christians who have said that sex is wrong, but as C. S. Lewis writes:

> Christianity is almost the only one of the great religions which thoroughly approves of the body . . . and nearly all the greatest love poetry in the world has been produced by Christians.
>
> (Mere Christianity)

Christians aren't prudes; they are people who accept and celebrate their sexuality—people who realize that making us male and female was one of the nicest things God has done for us.

Christians aren't playboys or playgirls either. They know that sex is more than a biological drive and they believe that restraint is necessary in every area of life. In fact, C. S. Lewis argues that because our sexual drive is so obviously inflamed and so easily twisted by sin, it especially needs restraint and careful handling.

So what attitude should Christians have toward sex? To understand sexuality properly, we must realize that there really is no such thing as sex. There are only sexual human beings. Sex is an abstraction; it does not exist by itself. We cannot slice a person into several different sections, call one of the sections *sex,* and have a relationship with it. Our sexuality is all wrapped up in our personalities, " . . . woven into the texture of our very being" (Lewis Smedes, *Sex For Christians*).

If we keep this in mind, we are not as likely to believe the illusion that television tries to sell us—the illusion that out there somewhere we shall find perfect sex. If we're looking for unending physical ecstasy, a relationship that is never marred by bad breath, hair curlers, or troubled conscience, we're going to be disappointed. This best-selling, Hollywood, no-worry sex does not exist. Only imperfect sexual human beings exist.

When Jerry first saw Ellen, he thought to himself: "If I could date her, I would never need to look at another girl. She's great!" The following day he called Ellen for a date and she accepted. Ecstasy!

He planned a perfect evening. Nothing could go wrong. And

everything *did* go fine except for Ellen's laugh. "Boy," Jerry thought, "for such a beautiful, delicate girl, she sure has a masculine laugh." It irritated him.

About a month and a half dozen dates later, Jerry couldn't help noticing a cold sore in the corner of Ellen's mouth, and he had to admit to himself that he was getting rather tired of hearing her talk about the school newspaper. Who cares?

It was in biology class the next day that Jerry met Mary, a new student at Fowler High. "Wow," he thought, "is she something!"

Ellen, Mary. . . the list of disappointments will continue to grow until Jerry realizes that sexuality is not dependent on physical perfection. The primary role of human sexuality is *communion*. Our sexuality attracts us toward the opposite sex on all levels: physically, emotionally, and spiritually. It seeks union. Dr. Smedes writes:

We experience our sexuality on the spiritual level as a yearning for another person. We want to reach out and stretch ourselves into the depths of another. We want to bring the other person into the orbit of our deepest selves. The physical yearning is meshed with the spiritual, and this is the total experience of sexual love.

(*Sex for Christians*)

How do we find this communion, this "total experience of sexual love"? Usually by progressing from random dating, to going steady, to engagement, to marriage. But this route is not without dangers.

For instance, there's the danger of superficial dating: having as much fun as possible, trying to impress the other person with how "neat" you are, but never really communicating. Certainly not every date has to be a profound experience in communion—and the younger we are the more casual we will want to be. Yet the important purpose of dating is to get to know each other.

Tony and Karen were probably the most handsome people in Anderson High. Tony was on the football team, and Karen was head cheerleader. The perfect couple. They rarely dated anyone else and were very quickly going steady. Everyone knew they would be married soon after high school graduation.

They were. But two years later their marriage was on the rocks and Karen filed for divorce. Good looks and high school sports did not make for a lasting union.

Before they got married, Karen and Tony hardly even knew each other.

If marriage means that two people promise each other to journey through life together, then dating has to be more than the superficial "I'm beautiful, you're beautiful" relationship of Karen and Tony. Through dating we have to make sure we are agreed on the direction and the purpose of the journey. As the father says to his daughter in *Fiddler on the Roof:* "A bird may love a fish, but where shall they build their home?" Basic compatibility is not learned under bed sheets, as some argue; it is learned as we discover each other's values and goals. As G. K. Chesterton once said: "If you want to know whether you will get along with your landlord, ask him what he thinks of God."

Another danger in the route from dating to marriage is the misuse of sexual intimacy. Let's agree that there's a real temptation to take advantage of each other in dating. We can use the other person. We can be wicked and insincere, pretending love and interest only to win sexual favors.

How do we avoid using others or being used? A principle which might prove helpful in this matter of intimacy is the principle of appropriateness: when some act is not clearly forbidden or obviously wrong—when within the area of morally permissible actions we still need guidance—then we might ask, "Is it appropriate?" For instance:

A young woman meets a young man at a party. A month later she sees him at the airport, rushes into his arms, and smothers him with kisses. Her action is inappropriate.

A husband comes home after a month-long business trip. His wife runs out to meet him and he greets her with a handshake. That action, too, is inappropriate.

Our sexual relationship must be in harmony with an overall intimacy. If we have gotten to first base together emotionally and spiritually, it is hardly appropriate to be running toward home plate physically. As far as the Bible is concerned, it is both very wrong and singularly inappropriate to give ourselves completely until we commit our heart and soul to one another in a permanent union called marriage.

That's the communion we were talking about earlier. Marriage—a lifelong relationship bound by promises and based on love, trust, loyalty, and shared goals. We pledge our love to each other as long as we *both* shall live. And because we are members of the community and because we easily go back on promises made in secret, we speak our vows publicly, in the presence of God, family, and friends. In the Song of Solomon the beloved says to her lover:

"Set me as a seal upon your heart, as a seal upon your arm" (8:6), which means: close your heart to every love but mine; hold no one in your arms but me. In marriage we make that promise.

It is in this context of complete trust and total commitment that we learn to give ourselves totally and joyously. So-called trial marriages are a contradiction; there is no marriage if the basic ingredients of trust and commitment are lacking. Couples who begin married life with the notion that divorce is a real option start with a terrible handicap. The moment any real difficulties arise between them, the idea of calling it quits starts to take shape.

To make a successful marriage we must be ready to pledge to each other the kind of love that Paul describes in I Corinthians 13. This is the love that:

> . . . is patient, [and] . . . kind. It does not envy, it does not boast, it is not proud. It is not rude, it is not self-seeking, it is not easily angered, it keeps no record of wrongs. . . . It always protects, always trusts, always hopes, always perseveres. (NIV)

In the Midst of Want

CHAPTER 8

Flora faced herself in the mirror. She hated what she saw—fat. She closed her eyes. "Oh, God," she breathed, "make the new pills work. Don't let me be fat anymore. Please don't. Being fat is the worst thing in the world."

May let

Mei-li found some grubs beneath a rock. Hurriedly she scratched them and ate them, getting as much dirt as grubs in her mouth. It was no matter—the dirt would fill her stomach too. The grubs only made the dirt go down easier.

Mrs. Foster looked at the cellophane-wrapped meat and asked, "Is this fresh? I mean *really* fresh?"

"Yes, ma'am. Sure is. I just cut it this afternoon," the butcher assured her.

Picking out a six-pound roast, Mrs. Foster put it in her cart and continued her rounds of the supermarket aisles. "Three dollars and twenty-eight cents a pound for a

Q. WHAT DOES GOD REQUIRE OF YOU IN THIS COMMANDMENT?

A. *That I do whatever I can*
  for my neighbor's good,
that I treat him
  as I would like others to treat me,
and that I work faithfully
  so that I may share with those in need.

Heidelberg Catechism, Q & A 111

seven-rib roast," she muttered to herself. "Outrageous! We've had to give up eating steak already! Humph! Somebody could make a million on a cookbook called *One Hundred Ways to Serve Ground Chuck.* I'd surely buy!"

Sighing, she continued to load up her cart, dreading the numbers that would pop up in the little window of the cash register.

Ma ree by Gowb

Marebi-Gaob doled out the grain to the women—a double handful for each house. He had learned to look at the eyes and not down at the swollen bellies—especially of the little ones. Although he was embarrassed to be giving so little grain into the eager hands, he was still thankful that there was enough grain left in the village store-house—perhaps enough so that each person would have at least one cake a day until those green shoots in the field matured and produced more. They would be all right then—if it didn't rain too much or too little, or if the river didn't overflow its banks, or if the insects didn't come, or if. . . .

(Adapted from G. William Jones, *The Innovator and Other Modern Parables**)

Flora and Mei-li, Mrs. Foster and Marebi-Gaob—their lives are as different as summer and winter, day and night. Yet they are citizens of the same planet. Why should some of earth's people have the luxury of complaining about their abundance while others cry out for enough? Why does such inequality exist? Why should Flora be fat while Mei-li eats dirt? These are questions no human being can ignore. They demand response. And yet many of us manage to shove them aside.

Perhaps the most common response to the cry of the hungry is indifference. One French journalist wrote, "If the third world is hungry, it is no business of mine. This is a fact for which I do not feel responsible, and therefore it does not interest me." Few of us would ever say that openly. Yet the sentiment comes fearfully close

to describing our lives. We are preoccupied with our own problems. Our concerns, even our prayers, embrace primarily ourselves and those nearest us. We isolate ourselves and give the unfortunate ones of our world only an occasional thought. "Like Lazarus at the rich man's door, the poor become. . . merely a part of the landscape to us. They may have all the crumbs they like, just so they make themselves scarce" (C. Plantinga Jr., *Beyond Doubt*).

Others respond not with indifference but with defensiveness. We've *earned* the privileges and favors we enjoy, they argue. We deserve what we have. This attitude is reflected in the following imaginary dialogue between the rich (our society) and the poor (the third world).

Rich: Why should we care about you? We have our own problems.

Poor: All the things you want for your country and your families, we would like to have, too. Are you the only ones that have a right to them? We have contributed to your development; don't you think it's time you contributed to ours?

Rich: But why don't you work harder? If you worked as hard as we have done, you'd get ahead.

Poor: You may have pulled yourselves up by your bootstraps but we don't have any straps, much less boots. We do work hard; often harder than you do. But many of us are hungry, malnourished, and sick. We aren't able to work as we would like. Then too, a lot of us can't find work. Our economies are struggling. Unemployment is high. Sometimes that unemployment is the result of trade policies of you rich nations that prevent us from competing in the international markets. We often don't have your tools or knowledge, and when you offer them to us, they may be too expensive or inappropriate for our conditions. Help us find new ways which are less complex and less expensive.

(W. S. Mooneyham,
"Christian Ethics in a Hungry World"*)

No doubt we have worked hard. But our success, the total package, includes so many factors over which we have no control. We cannot take personal credit for our food, our education, our opportunities, or our intelligence.

Yet many persist in believing that we somehow have a *right* to our designer jeans, summer homes, and winter trips to Acapulco. Some of these, of course, feel an occasional twinge of conscience. That's the group (and it may include many of us) who respond with the occasional handout. One writer calls it the "beggar's mentality": in the presence of suffering we are a soft touch; we quickly reach into our pockets to still our conscience. But our lives remain unchanged. We show no real interest in the day-to-day living of the weak and the poor.

Then there are those of us who *are* interested in the plight of the world's poor and needy. We are touched by pictures of starving children, by stories of the boat people fleeing communist persecution, by thousands of Cubans swarming into Florida. Yet we don't know how to really help these people, to change the conditions which cause their poverty. They are often half a world away . . . and there seems to be so little we can do. So we adopt a defeatist attitude: "What's the use? There's nothing we can do."

Obviously, none of these responses—indifference, defensiveness, occasional handouts, or defeatism—is the right response for Christians. Clearly the Bible demands active concern. The psalmist writes: "Defend the rights of the poor and the orphan; be fair to the needy and the helpless" (82:3). In Isaiah we are told: ". . . If you spend yourselves on behalf of the hungry and satisfy the needs of the oppressed, then your light will rise in the darkness, and your light will become like the noonday" (58:10, NIV). These and dozens of other biblical commands leave no doubt about the Christian's responsibility: we must actively work for justice, practice stewardship of personal and national wealth, and accept the responsibility God has given us to guard our neighbors' good.

Why justice for all? Why should we bother giving each person his or her due? Because all human beings, including the dull-witted classmate and the hungry child in Bangladesh,

*From *Christian Social Ethics*, edited by Perry C. Cotham, Baker Book House, 1979. Used by permission.

are made in the likeness of God. And as image-bearers, invaluable and precious to God, they have the right to be treated as persons.

Treating others as persons involves more than superficial courtesy. Since every person is called by God to develop his or her gifts and abilities and to perform a task in the world, justice demands that he or she be given both the freedom and the opportunity to obey this call. Social conditions that rob a person of his or her ability to be obedient to God's calling should be changed. Unnecessary obstacles and unfair hindrances to human development ought to be removed whenever possible. At the very least this means that every person should have enough food to eat.

Imagine ten children at a table dividing up food. The three healthiest load their plates with large portions, including most of the meat, fish, milk, and eggs. They eat what they want and discard the leftovers. Two other children get just enough to meet their basic requirements. The remaining five are left wanting. Three of them—sickly, nervous, apathetic children—manage to stave off the feeling of hunger by filling up on bread and rice. The other two cannot even do that.

One dies from dysentery and the second from pneumonia, which they are too weak to ward off.

(Arthur Simon,
Bread for the World)

We, the people of the United States and Canada, are like those three healthy children. Unless we begin to seek justice, five of the other children, or half the world's population, may sicken or die.

How can we seek justice for those other "children"? By practicing stewardship. Some people think stewardship means it's wrong to make money—especially a lot of money. That's not true. In the same way that it is not immoral to be highly intelligent or very popular, it is not immoral to make money—as long as it's done honestly. Stewardship involves what we *do* with that money. It involves remembering that we have no absolute ownership, but are in all things accountable to God. All of our wealth is his. For that reason, a Christian steward must honestly ask: how much may I spend on myself and on what may I spend it?

. . . Most of us spend more than we need to on luxury items. We take them for granted. We eat a lot of junk food, drink a lot of expensive beverages, become clothes racks for whatever designers want us to wear, travel well and far, and surround ourselves with comforts. Every such expenditure must be made with the knowledge that as we make it hundreds of human creatures of God keel over and die from starvation.

(C. Plantinga Jr., Beyond Doubt, Leader's Guide)

In spite of that knowledge, we spend. We are addicted consumers. It's so easy to go along with society's assumption that as a person's income increases so does the size of his or her house, car, boat, cottage, and what not. But the Christian must not share this assumption. The fact that we are bright and not dumb, rich and not poor, healthy and not sickly must be understood primarily in terms of responsibility and service—not privilege. And in the midst of want we must be modest in our wants.

We have a responsibility to be good stewards and to seek justice. We have a responsibility to hungry people. Obviously we cannot be responsible for the *whole* world. Our responsibility is limited by our ability. God will not ask a blind man to rush into a burning house to save a child, but he may ask it of us who have two good eyes. In this world of want there are clearly a great many things we cannot do. We cannot answer every appeal for help. We cannot be a friend to every friendless person in the school or church. We cannot change the international trade policies of our country—though our voice, joined to thousands and even millions of other voices, is bound to be noticed by the government.

However, instead of emphasizing our limits, we need to stress our responsibility. Most of us are still inclined to ignore our neighbor in trouble. We are constantly tempted to pass by on the other side—like the priest and the Levite in Jesus' parable of the Good Samaritan. Unless we realize our obligations and respond to the world's poor, we may be among those who live sixty or seventy years on this earth and in the end exclaim, "When did we see you hungry or thirsty or lonely or sick?"

Though we cannot change the world, we *can* change our own lives and be more sensitive to those in need. Though we cannot change the life-style of a wasteful, throw-away society, we *can* do something about our own habits. Though we cannot make the other students kind toward the friendless, we *can* be a friend. Our little light may not shatter the darkness throughout the universe, but it can cast some light into the immediate surroundings. And our influence for good may just surprise us.

Tongue-tied?

CHAPTER 9

"*. . . no human being can tame the tongue—
a restless evil, full of deadly poison.*"

James 3:8

Marjoe, "the world's tiniest shepherd," began his career as an evangelist at the tender age of three. By the time he was four he was famous. Everyone was talking about the four-year-old preacher who stirred up headline news and a legal ruckus by performing a wedding ceremony in Long Beach, California.

For the next ten years Marjoe hit the revival trail deep in the Southern Bible Belt. Shouting, frantically waving his arms, strutting the stage, pounding the pulpit, the child evangelist exhorted his congregations to give the devil two black eyes and to follow Jesus.

Marjoe was a wonder child, a little curly-haired evangelist with the voice and looks of an angel, and the talents and training of a child actor. Before he was six he had memorized fourteen sermons, enough for two weeks in one town. He had almost as many costumes and, depending on the sermon title, turned up dressed as a cowboy, a drum major, or a good shepherd. The sermons were carefully choreographed by his mother, Sister Marge. Every movement, gesture, and word was practiced for hours in front of a full-length mirror. In some sermons he could take longer to say "Gaaawwwd" with both arms outstretched than it normally took him to say, "I'm here to give the devil two black eyes."

Sitting closely behind him in the pulpit, Sister Marge would gauge the audience and call out cue words to keep Marjoe on track. "Hallelujah" meant hurry up, you're dragging; "Glory" was slow down, and "Praise God" or "Thank You, Jesus" meant take the offering.

Marjoe soon learned that the offering was the cornerstone of every service. While his parents stood at the altar calling for money, he would run up and down the aisles stuffing bills into his suits, sometimes being obliged to kiss all the ladies who gave over $20. Marjoe figures the family took in close to $3 million in the first eight years of his ministry.

(Hal Wingo,
"The Confessions of Marjoe," *Life*)

In 1972 the adult Marjoe made a documentary film to confess his "sins." The film, entitled *Marjoe,* is a kaleidoscope of old film clippings, tracing the young evangelist's early career and focusing on his last months of preaching. "I can't think of a time that I even believed in God or thought it was a miracle of God that I preached," Marjoe admits to the viewer. "I just knew I could do it well."

What are his feelings about his deceitful past? "I'm bad," Marjoe admits, "but I'm not evil." Perhaps, as one of the film's critics speculates, Marjoe has the mistaken impression that he and only he was harmed by the lie that he lived. Nothing could be further from the truth: few sins are done in such isolation that they touch no one but the sinner. To understand the extent of the damage done by Marjoe's lies, imagine the spiritual trauma of those people taken in by his rip-off revival services. Will they ever be able to trust preachers or their own spiritual feelings again? And if not, what has replaced their faith?

Probably skepticism. As revelations like Marjoe's become more and more common, skepticism, like an acid, eats away at the pillars of trust in our society. Those we have respected and those who appear to be honest, are proven liars and we begin to doubt everything we hear—even the truth. Is there an energy shortage—or not? Does the politician intend to keep the promises he made on the campaign trail—or was he just trying to get votes? Did our government support the overthrow of another nation's government—or is that just rumor?

What the news media, political leaders, teachers, and even ministers say is up for grabs in today's society: maybe it's true—but maybe it's not. We have heard so many lies, so many confessions like Marjoe's, that we find it difficult to recognize the truth. And, because "everyone else is doing it," we find it easier and easier to lie.

Easier, that is, until we listen to God. As Christians we are forbidden to lie. When we speak, we are to tell the truth. The psalmist tells us God desires "truth in the inner parts" (Ps. 51:6, NIV); everything false, phony, and hypocritical must be banished. In speech and in action we are to be fully trustworthy.

Does that mean it's never permissible for a Christian to lie, even under extreme circumstances? Although some Christians would say yes, most would agree that in certain situations a lie is justified and thoroughly defendable. This position has its hazards. Once we defend a lie, we usually find it easier to excuse another. And we gradually fall into a pattern which we call "telling little white lies." All of us have heard and probably told white lies—those trivial, seemingly harmless little "falsehoods" told with good intentions.

Joe asked Amy for a date. Amy had nothing planned for Friday, but the idea of spending a whole evening with Joe hardly appealed to her. And so Amy told him she had to babysit. The white lie seemed kinder to her than the truth.

Henry forgot to set his alarm and was a half hour late for work. When he saw his boss's frowning face, Henry explained that he had to wait thirty minutes at a train crossing. The white lie got Henry out of a scrape.

Lucille smiled sweetly at her hostess. "What a lovely dress," she complimented. Actually she thought the color was ghastly and the style out of the dark ages. But she was pleased to see that her white lie had flattered the woman. If there's anything Lucille hated, it was offending one of her friends.

Little white lies, completely harmless, said with the best intentions—we do it all the time. "All the same, it is possible that most of our white lies are told, not for charity, but for laziness and for cowardice—to save the work of thinking up a real answer, or to avoid a trivial social discomfort" (Joy Davidman, *Smoke on the Mountain*).

Telling the truth is a very serious duty. That doesn't mean we have to be brutally honest: Amy would have accomplished more harm than good, for example, by saying, "Joe, I would rather spend an evening picking lint off my socks than go out with you." But we can't thoughtlessly tell the white lie just to avoid a tense situation either. We must maintain an attitude of respect and concern for others, telling the truth *in love*.

Furthermore, it is doubtful whether the "harmless little white lie" is really so harmless. Consider what would happen if everyone shaded unpleasant truths with lies.

Suppose you are a teacher who is asked to write a letter of recommendation for one of your students, Joyce. You lie by highly exaggerating Joyce's qualifications. You happen to like her and know she needs a job badly.

Your motive is good, and you feel the lie is harmless. But is it?

Another student, Kathy, equally qualified, applies for the same job. Her recommendation, however, is accurate and straightforward. Because of your inflated recommendation, Kathy loses a fair chance at the job.

Kathy and many others like her become victims of careless white lies—lies told for convenience or comfort. As Christians we can't justify lying for such motives and circumstances. In fact, the *one legitimate reason* the Christian may use for telling a lie is that telling the truth would bring serious harm. In a war, for example, a lie may be necessary to protect the lives of others. Or a doctor may find it necessary to lie about a patient's condition for fear that the truth would cause a heart attack. Or . . .

Y ou have become President of the United States of America. Automatically, you are commander-in-chief of all the armed forces; at your disposal is the total destructive power of the nation's nuclear stockpile. You have concluded, however, after a great deal of soul-searching, that morally you could not be party to the total destruction that would be unleashed in an all-out nuclear war. Of course, you do not make this conclusion public. You realize that that kind of talk would eliminate nuclear weapons as a deterrent to a hostile foe, greatly encourage aggression, and very likely create war.

On the contrary, you tell the world that you will not hesitate to use all the military power of the nation to defend the interests of the free world.

Your enemies believe that you will use nuclear bombs to the degree that they are ready to use such weapons. As the old proverb says: we paint others with the same brush that we paint ourselves. Your lie discourages enemies from making a hostile move.

Even though we might justify a lie in such extreme situations, as a last resort, we must underscore caution. It is extremely easy to persuade ourselves that a lie is totally necessary. Therefore, before we allow the deception to occur, we ought to test ourselves and the reasons for telling it.

First, is our conscience, that inner judge, wholly at peace with the justification for the lie?

Second, would we justify this lie before a public gathering of morally sensitive men and women from various walks of life? Would we, for example, be embarrassed to appear on the 11 o'clock news and explain why we lied?

Third, would we argue any differently if the lie were told to us? In other words, how would we feel if this deceptive practice were played on us? Always apply the "golden rule."

Fourth, are we doing everything possible to change the conditions that made the lie necessary? Even when the doctor lies for the patient's good, he or she must make every effort to help the patient finally face the truth.

Because communication is one of God's finest gifts to us, we must guard it with the truth. As the Heidelberg Catechism says: God requires that

> . . . in court and everywhere else,
> I should avoid lying and deceit of every kind;
>> these are devices the devil himself uses,
>> and they would call down on me God's intense anger.
> I should love the truth,
>> speak it candidly,
>> and openly acknowledge it.
> And I should do what I can
>> to guard and advance my neighbor's good name.

(Answer 112)

AND YET

CHAPTER 10

It wasn't that Jake was bad looking; he wasn't. But physically he was definitely a late bloomer—and he hated it. When he was in the seventh grade, he was so short that the barber still had to give him a special booster stool to sit on. How Jake despised that stool.

He kept hoping that a miracle would happen—that he would grow twelve inches and gain fifty pounds and start looking his age. But when Jake entered high school, people were still making a big deal about how young he looked. Even when he grew a few inches and didn't need the barber's stool anymore, he still looked like a kid.

Jake was miserable. Girls didn't notice he was around, and it was no wonder. He looked like one of his classmate's younger brother. In gym class he felt more like a mascot than a participant. And when he saw some of the other guys shaving, he really got depressed. No matter how hard he stared into the mirror, he could only find a hair here and a hair there. There was more fuzz on a canned peach! And it didn't help to learn that his father hardly shaved at all, even when he was in the army.

Jake wished with all his heart that he would look more his age. He often prayed about it.

Like Jake, we want to be happy. And like Jake, many of us are convinced that we've been shortchanged. Either we're too short or too tall, too fat or too thin, too shy or too bold. We spend our time dwelling on dozens of "if only's": if only I had more money; if only I had a car; if only I looked like Burt Reynolds (or Cheryl Tiegs); if only I got all A's. If only . . . then I'd be happy for sure.

What many of us don't realize is that most of these "if only's" come from comparing ourselves to others. We may be perfectly happy with our appearance or our wardrobe until we notice that others are better looking and better dressed than we are. Then dissatisfaction sets in. And in most cases we remain dissatisfied until what we have is bigger and better than our neighbor's.

Aesop, the Greek writer of fables, tells the story of a man to whom the gods promised anything he wished. The man could hardly believe his good fortune. There was, however, one catch: his every wish would come true only on the condition that his neighbor would get twice as much of whatever it was he wished for. The thought of his neighbor's good luck, always doing him one better, spoiled his happy mood. What good was the wish if it didn't make him better off than his neighbor? He thought and thought, and suddenly a smile crossed his face. He had it—the perfect wish! Grinning smugly, he told the gods he wished to lose one eye.

Few of us would wish away an eye to compete with a neighbor, but the fact remains that we are very concerned with how our gifts and possessions measure up to everyone elses'. We get so wrapped up in the external circumstances of life that we assume our happiness depends on good looks, popularity, and wealth.

That assumption is false. Life's circumstances do, of course, make a difference. Certainly we with healthy bodies should have an easier time being content and happy than the person struggling with cerebral palsy. And the person who says that money is not important is either a fool or a millionaire. Money *is* important: it can buy services (your education) and comforts that are both extremely useful and enjoyable.

Nevertheless, good health and a million dollars are not a guarantee of happiness. The healthy millionaire struggles with her own "if only's." The football hero envies the class president. The valedictorian wants to look like the homecoming queen. As long as we link our happiness to things—like money and popularity—we will discover that we never have quite enough, that there is always something to disturb our peace and make us want more.

Eddie stood in the front yard and watched the big boys walking to school.

"When I get to be six I'll go to school, and it will be very nice," he said.

But when Eddie got to be six and did go to school, it wasn't all that nice.

"When I go to high school it'll be keen," Eddie said, dreaming of being a football star, driving his own jalopy, and of having big muscles under his letter sweater.

But when Ed did go to high

school, things didn't work out the way he planned.

"When I get out of this dumb place," he said with disgust, "I'm going to the University, where they treat you like an adult. It won't be boring, and the girls are too mature to care whether or not you're a football star."

The University didn't quite work out the way Ed planned either.

"Well," he said, "life is really going to begin when I graduate, get a good job, and have my own apartment."

But life didn't seem to get started too well, even when Ed found a pretty good job and had a much too expensive apartment all to himself.

"I'm so lonely," he said. "That's what's wrong. Just about everything that's wrong with my life now would be solved if I had a good wife."

Marriage did solve a lot of Ed's problems, but it created a few more—like money problems, for instance.

"Just think how it'd be if I got that promotion," Ed chortled to his wife. "We could get a second car, go to Bermuda for our vacations, and even buy a house with a bedroom for each of the kids!"

But when Ed finally did get that promotion, the bigger income was soon swallowed up in bigger bills, and he was under just as much financial strain as ever. And with his new responsibilities he was under greater psychological pressure at the office. No, the promotion didn't make life happen.

"Life will really be wonderful," Edward mused as he looked searchingly at the gray at his temples in the mirror, "when I retire. I'll still be relatively young, and I can fish, hunt—be free of responsibilities."

Edward retired. He was out in his new boat one day, heading for a spot where the lodge's proprietor had assured him he'd have no trouble catching a six-or eight-pound bass.

"All my life I've been looking for happiness and contentment," he thought as the boat slid across the water. "When I get used to this retirement way of life, I think it's finally going to be great!"

Of course, by now he didn't

really believe that. That's why he added (to reassure himself), "Now, for the first time, I feel that life—real living—is just around the corner!"

With a searing pain in his chest, Edward turned that corner. And there it was, waiting for him. No, not life—death.

With that he dropped the whole matter.

(G. William Jones,
*The Innovator and
Other Modern Parables**)

The Christian life must not be, like Edward's, a continual longing for the bigger, better, richer tomorrow. We must learn contentment. We must learn that happiness and our worth as individuals are not tied up with the fortunes and misfortunes of life. But that is not an easy lesson. In a society geared toward consumerism and success, contentment seems strangely out of place. Actually, it is the only road to happiness.

How do we learn to be content? First, by developing a sane and realistic attitude toward the prices and rewards that life holds out to us. We must not believe those who tell us that we will find paradise just over the next hill—with this purchase or in that romance. As long as we think that a change in our appearance or in our social status can bring us true and lasting happiness, we shall covet it and be embittered if it escapes our grasp.

Secondly, we must keep a distance between our possessions and our true value as human beings. As long as what we possess props up our soul, gives meaning to our life, we will clutch it as if our very life depended on it. We will always want more of it—and dread losing it.

The apostle Paul advises that we keep a certain detachment from our possessions. We should possess nothing we could not do without. Perhaps our attitude toward our belongings ought to be something like the attitude we take in playing a game of Monopoly. You are a serious player; you intend to play your best; but you keep in mind that it's just a game. You do not weep uncontrollably if you land on Boardwalk, even with a hotel on it. And you would certainly not cheat or sacrifice your morals to get out of paying the owner of Boardwalk.

This does not mean that you take the game lightly—those who do are poor players—but neither do you take it too seriously, as if it were the only thing that mattered. Players who do that, besides everything else, are extremely poor losers. To be a good player you need to take the game seriously and yet not too seriously.

Actually, few of us can remain as detached from our own health, wealth, and appearance as we do from the outcome of a Monopoly game— but it is something to strive for. And we don't have to do the striving all alone. The apostle Paul lets us know that contentment isn't out of reach. He himself found contentment—in Christ.

There is our clue. Contentment comes not from fame and fortune; contentment comes from being so taken in by Christ's love that everything else is secondary. It's the *only* way. A dog will growl and snarl when you try to take the dry, sun-bleached bone away from her. But throw her a steak and she gives up the bone without a fight.

Christians find their worth in belonging to God. It may sound trite and, at times, it may come out that way. Yet what can we really compare to having seen for ourselves God's hand outstretched to us and holding ours? Dr. Lewis Smedes says this gives the Christian *poise*. He writes:

> The word "poise" originally referred to the weight placed in the center of a sailing ship for balance. This. . .[weight] set the keel deep enough into the water to keep the ship from capsizing. By ourselves, without God, we are too light at the center; we are like ships without *poise*, likely to capsize. We boast and become rude and arrogant, in the hope that praise from others will act as external braces to make up for lack of centered weight. It is God's love that can give us centered weight on the inside.
>
> As the love of God keeps coming into us

from the outside, we can forget about our emptiness and move on to others.

> (Lewis Smedes, *Love Within Limits*)

And with God as the center of our life, we can begin the hard task of facing the reality of who and what we are—looking at our limitations honestly and unflinchingly, and then striving for excellence.

The story is told of a sky diver. On his nineteenth jump his parachute failed to open fully, and his emergency chute wrapped itself around the main chute. He slammed into a dry lake bed at sixty miles an hour. Doctors thought he would never leave the hospital. They told him so, and the man sank into a deep despair.

Another patient in that hospital, a man whose spinal cord had been broken in an automobile accident, often visited the sky diver. This patient had his own problems. He would never walk again; in fact, he would never move a finger again. But he was always cheerful. "I certainly don't recommend my situation to anyone," he would say, "*and yet* I can read, I can listen to music, I can talk to people."

(Adapted from Arthur Gordon, *A Touch of Wonder*)

And yet. The two words shift our focus from what we do not have to what is ours and what may still be gained. Apathy does not distinguish between what can and cannot be changed; acceptance does. There may be things that we do not have and will never have, *and yet* we are God's children and he expects that we do our very best for him with what we do have.

CLIMBING THE MOUNTAIN

CHAPTER 11

Let us not become weary in doing good. . . .
Galatians 6:9, NIV

The geese gathered twice every Sunday. They were very religious geese and they very much enjoyed the preaching of the elder gander. And truly, it was a delight how that gander could preach. What a gift! Every sermon was spoken with just the right blend of eloquence and plain talk, and no matter from what text he began he always ended by telling the flock that their Creator had made them for a greater, more glorious land. With a voice that strained under the weight of such magnificent news he told them that the Creator had given them wings with which they would one day fly away to a far country, a blessed country, where they would be at home at last. It wouldn't be an easy flight, he warned them. They would have to train their wings and practice their flying if they expected to be in top condition when the great day came.

Meanwhile the geese lived well. They enjoyed plenty of food and plenty of sunshine. And eventually they grew fat. If the truth were told, except for Sunday, they thought very little about that great journey and that blessed country. "We have it good," one would say, lazily stretching herself out in the sun. "Yes," another would reply, "we've been blessed."

Of course, there were some exceptions. Here and there a few geese took the gander's message seriously. They thought about flying all week long, made practice runs, encouraged others to join them in their practice. What pests they were. And they looked so thin and ill that it led one goose to say, "You see—that's what happens when your mind is always on flying. You get thin and don't thrive. Being plump and fat and tender is a sign of our Creator's blessing."

Weeks passed into months. One day, without warning, winter came. Snow covered the green grass and gray clouds hid the sun. The fat geese huddled together wondering what to do. They waited for the elder gander to give them some advice. But they weren't prepared for what they heard. "It's time," the elder gander said happily, "to leave for the blessed country." With that he began to flap his strong well-practiced wings and rose into the air, calling his flock to follow.

Those who could—the few who practiced daily—did. They took to the air in beautiful formation. The rest fluttered and floundered on the ground. They had never tried their wings before and now found their attempts to fly futile. Their wings were too weak, their bodies too fat—they fainted from exhaustion ten feet from the ground.

So while the elder gander and his few followers flew off toward the blessed country, the fat geese, shivering in the cold, waddled back to their shelters.

(Adapted from Søren Kierkegaard, *The Last Years**)

Like the fat geese, we are often more willing to listen than to do. On Sunday, we hear that we are pilgrims and that this world is a training ground, a place where we learn how to walk with God. We nod our heads solemnly as the preacher describes our glorious future with God—but on Monday and Tuesday we're often so different. We treat the world like an amusement park or a marketplace and not at all like a training ground.

The geese gained nothing from their two Sunday gatherings because they never practiced the flying which the elder gander preached. It's the same way with us. Sermons on Sunday and courses in decision making will benefit us only if we make an effort to be holy in *all* our living, not just on Sunday. All the courses on morality in the world will not help us be Christians unless we're willing to practice that morality daily—even when it seems unprofitable or uncomfortable.

Some people make the mistake of thinking that Christian living is primarily a means of getting ahead in this life. Like the fat geese they pat themselves on the back for attending church twice on Sunday and talk smugly about how they've "been blessed." They bargain with God, hoping to exchange a donation and a little devotion for a promotion, faithful church attendance for better grades. Actually their dream is no different than the rest of the world's—they want a comfortable, trouble-free place under the sun. And they figure that because they have "faith," God owes them success. One television evangelist often ends his prayers by saying something like:

And I pray that as I stretch forth these hands which I've given to God, that a miracle in your finances, in your health, in

*Adapted from pp. 292-293 in *The Last Years* by Søren Kierkegaard, edited and translated by Ronald Gregor Smith. © 1965 by Ronald Gregor Smith. Reprinted by permission of Harper & Row Publishers, Inc.

your marriage, and in your relationships with people will begin to happen *now*, this very day, at this very moment. Amen and Amen.

(Jerry Sholes,
Give Me That Prime-Time Religion)

Of course, some Christians *will* experience miracles in their finances, their health, or their marriages. Some Christians will be very successful in this world. But Christ never promised his disciples a rose garden. He never guaranteed a fat bankroll and popularity as rewards for faith. What he did make very clear is that following him would *not* be easy. He commanded us to take up our crosses and follow him—not just when it's convenient, but always.

Following Christ can be very trying. There is every chance that we become weary of doing good and tired of being Christians.

Joan was a homely girl and not very bright. She was a loser and she didn't have the good sense to fade into the woodwork. She was loud. No wonder she didn't have any friends. People avoided her as much as possible.

In a conversation with members of the Young People's Society, Joan's pastor suggested they make a real effort to include Joan in their activities. They promised to try.

Since Bob lived near Joan, he began picking her up on Thursday nights for the society meeting. Joan couldn't believe her good fortune; nor could she keep it quiet. Soon half the school was wondering what was going on between Bob and Joan. Whenever she saw Bob coming down the hall with some of his friends, Joan would wave and say—so everyone could hear—"Hi, Bobby!"

Bob could hardly bear it. He had to keep reminding himself of what the pastor had said about Joan's problems and her loneliness. But at times he found himself almost hating her. And he didn't know how much longer he could keep his promise to the pastor.

Taking up our cross may mean being kind to the Joans of this world—even when it hurts. It may mean doing many things that are unpleasant, boring, embarrassing, or tiring. We need not apply for Christian discipleship if we want a life of ease. Yet once we take up the cross, we'll find that in spite of hardship and pain, following Christ is the one thing that gives our lives meaning.

Imagine a huge mountain. You are near the bottom of that mountain, struggling toward the very top. As you climb, you meet someone who has given up the climb and is on her way down. She sees you struggling and says to you: "If you would throw aside that large sign you have on your back, you would find climbing much easier.

"Drop the sign?" you ask in surprise. "But I am climbing in order to post this sign at the top. Without this sign there would be no reason to climb the mountain."

(Adapted from Martin Buber, *A Believing Humanism*)

Christian living is like that. At times, like the sign on the climber's back, it seems to make life much more difficult. It would be so much easier to cheat and lie and do whatever is necessary to get ahead. But without the sign, without Christian morality, the whole climb loses its purpose.

Naturally, even after we've taken up our sign—our Christian way of life—we try different ways to get around the steep demands of the gospel. Sometimes we argue that since we are saved by grace and not by our works, we can take the easy route. At other times, we try to reduce the struggle of the climb by cutting the mountain down to our size. We try to convince ourselves that all Christ really demands is a decent, respectable showing in life. Often we argue for the low road by telling ourselves that what we are and do is really not so important.

In a world of over four billion people and in a universe so immense that the nearest star is billions of miles away, does it really make any difference whether or not I cheat on an exam or sleep with my boyfriend? People do it all the time. And when they get older they sit in church and become elders and deacons. Besides, I can always repent afterwards; the pastor keeps saying God forgives. There is no need to be serious about being good.

None of the above arguments, however, will find any support in the Bible. Christ demands our very best. Once we've begun the climb, there is no idle loafing and no time out. This doesn't mean we will reach the summit in a day or even in a lifetime. Most of us are not very good climbers. But then, Christ's primary concern is not how high we climb the mountain, but whether we're heading the right way and doing our very best. Our poor showing only underscores our need for Jesus Christ, the perfect climber.

And even with his help, the climb will be strenuous. Others may wonder what makes us continue—why don't we "drop the sign." The answer is simple: we keep going out of gratitude—out of sheer wonder at what God in Christ has done for us. We strive to live God-pleasing lives to say thanks. Our primary aim is not to become good people, but to show our thankfulness for Christ's sacrifice. And in this self-forgetting quest, we climb the mountain of holiness.

Dr. James Stewart tells the story of a traveler in Africa who visits a hospital. He sees a nun dressing the gruesome wounds of a leper. In total repulsion he says: "I wouldn't do that if you paid me ten thousand dollars." The nun looks up and replies: "I wouldn't either."

Like the traveler, most non-Christians will be mystified by the things we do—not for fame or money or success, but out of gratitude. We Christians always entertain the hope that these others will see Christ in us and leave the valley to join the climb up the mountain. Few things speak more convincingly about the beauty of Christ than beautiful lives. In the New Testament we learn that:

> St. Thomas . . . believed some things, but he did not . . . believe Christ's resurrection. Then Christ gave him His body to be the proof: and He gives *us* His body to be the proof. Christ's body is still in the world, His body is His faithful people.
>
> It was not every part of Christ's body that equally convinced St. Thomas, it was the parts that carried the prints of the crucifixion. And it is not every part of Christ's body that now convinces us, it is the crucified parts: not every . . . common Christian, but the saints who are marked with the signs of Christ's sacrifice. There are such men (and women) in the world, and we have known them: men whose words are like their faces and their faces like their hearts, and their hearts printed with the cross of Jesus.
>
> (Austin Farrer, *The End of Man*)

The world must know that we are Christians by our love. May we let our light shine before people so that they will see our good works and praise our Father in heaven (Matt. 5:16).

BIBLIOGRAPHY

Allen, Charles. *God's Psychiatry.* New York: Pyramid Books, 1964.

Anderson, Norman. *Issues of Life and Death.* Downers Grove, Ill.: Intervarsity Press, 1978.

Barclay, William. *The Ten Commandments for Today.* New York: Harper & Row Pubs., 1973.

Barth, Karl. *Church Dogmatics,* vol. III/4. Edinburg: T & T Clark, 1961.

Bok, Sisela. *Lying: Moral Choice in Public and Private Life.* New York: Vintage Books, 1979.

Brooks, Phillip. *The Light of the World and Other Sermons.* New York: E. P. Dutton & Co., 1910.

Brown, Robert Mc Afee. *The Bible Speaks to You.* Philadelphia: Westminster Press, 1955.

Buber, Martin. *A Believing Humanism.* New York: Simon and Schuster, 1969.

Davidman, Joy. *Smoke on the Mountain.* Philadelphia: Westminster Press, 1954.

Dobson, James. *Dare to Discipline.* Wheaton, Ill.: Tyndale House, 1972.

————. *Hide or Seek.* Old Tappan, N.J.: Fleming H. Revell Co., 1974.

Farrer, Austin. *A Faith of Our Own.* New York: World Publishing Co., 1960.

————. *The End of Man.* Grand Rapids: Wm. B. Eerdmans Pub. Co., 1974.

Gheddo, Piero. *Why is the Third World Poor?* Maryknoll, N.Y.: Orbis Books, 1973.

Gordon, Arthur. *A Touch of Wonder.* Old Tappan, N.J.: Fleming H. Revell Co., 1974.

Hallie, Philip. *Lest Innocent Blood Be Shed.* New York: Harper & Row Pubs., 1979.

Jones, Rufus M. *New Eyes for Invisibles.* New York: The Macmillan Co., 1944.

Jones, William G. *The Innovator and Other Modern Parables.* New York: Abingdon Press, 1969.

Kierkegaard, Søren. *The Last Years.* Edited by Ronald G. Smith. New York: Harper & Row Pubs. 1965.

Lewis, Clive Staples. *Mere Christianity.* New York: The Macmillan Co., 1978.

Mooneyham, Stanley W. "Christian Ethics in a Hungry World." In *Christian Social Ethics.* Edited by Perry C. Cotham. Grand Rapids: Baker Book House, 1979.

Morgan, Campbell G. "The Training of Our Children." In *The Westminster Pulpit,* vol. II. Old Tappan, N.J.: Fleming H. Revell Co., 1954.

Muggeridge, Malcolm. *Something Beautiful for God.* London: Collins, 1973.

Olthuis, James H. *I Pledge You My Troth.* New York: Harper & Row Pubs., 1975.

Plantinga, Cornelius Jr. *Beyond Doubt.* Grand Rapids, Board of Publications of the Christian Reformed Church, 1980.

————. *A Place to Stand.* Grand Rapids: Board of Publications of the Christian Reformed Church, 1979.

Ramsey, Paul. *The Patient as Person.* New Haven: Yale University Press, 1970.

Ruggiero, Vincent R. *The Moral Imperative.* Port Washington, N.Y.: Alfred Publishing Co. Inc., 1973.

Russell, Bertrand. "A Free Man's Worship." In *Readings for Liberal Education.* Edited by G. Arms, W. Gibson, and L. Locke. New York: Holt, Rinehart, & Winston, 1962.

Sholes, Jerry. *Give Me that Prime-time Religion.* New York: Hawthorn Books, 1979.

Simon, Arthur. *Bread for the World.* Grand Rapids: Wm. B. Eerdmans Pub. Co., 1975.

Smedes, Lewis. *Love Within Limits.* Grand Rapids: Wm. B. Eerdmans Pub. Co., 1978.

————. *Sex For Christians.* Grand Rapids: Wm. B. Eerdmans Pub. Co., 1976.

————. "Theology and the Prayerful Life." In *God and the Good.* Edited by C. Orlebeke and L. Smedes. Grand Rapids: Wm. B. Eerdmans Pub. Co., 1975.

Steinbeck, John. *Travels with Charley.* New York: Bantam Books, 1963.

Stob, Henry. *Ethical Reflections.* Grand Rapids: Wm. B. Eerdmans Pub. Co., 1978.

Thielicke, Helmut. *Theological Ethics*, vol. 1 & 2. Philadelphia: Fortress Press, 1969.

Trueblood, Elton. *Foundations for Reconstruction.* New York: Harper & Row Pubs., 1946.